PARIS
AIRPORTS

PARIS
AIRPORTS

ORLY
CHARLES DE GAULLE
LE BOURGET

Airlife
England

Contents

Foreword	4
Acknowledgements	5
History	6
Orly	18
Charles de Gaulle	52
Le Bourget	92
Aerodromes of Paris	110
Foreign Airports	112
Maps	116
Traffic Figures	120

Aram Gesar

Foreword

Since the dawn of air travel, Paris has witnessed many heroic successes and historic events, carried out by such illustrious pioneers as Louis Blériot and Charles Lindbergh.

But the theatres of those exploits of long ago have changed and the original airfield has become an airport and instead of the adventure of the air we now have the air transport industry, full of ambition and promise.

Nowadays, a modern airport has all the features of a vast industrial and commercial centre. Its management has become a huge undertaking that has to provide airlines and their passengers with the most effective infrastructures and services possible. The importance of air transport in a particular region is sometimes so great that several airports and aerodromes need to be managed by a single airport authority. And this is the case with Paris, where no less than 14 such facilities are under the authority of "Aéroports de Paris" (ADP). These 14 are:

- Orly and Roissy-Charles de Gaulle, two large airports dedicated to commercial traffic;
- Le Bourget, which is now a business aviation airport, well-known for its Air Museum and for being the site of the International Air and Space Fair;
- Chavenay, Chelles, Coulommiers, Etampes, Lognes, Meaux, Persan, Pontoise, Saint-Cyr, and Toussus-le-Noble: ten aerodromes used for activities such as business and leisure flying, and flying schools;
- Paris-Issy-les-Moulineaux: a heliport.

With such an air transport system, which is among the most comprehensive and efficient in the world, Paris is a real economic crossroads of the air transport industry. The network served by the 142 airlines that regularly fly to and from the capital connects it to 510 towns and cities in 135 countries. In 1995, Orly and Roissy-Charles de Gaulle handled 55 million passengers and 1.2 million tons of freight and mail. Paris is unquestionably one of the most active airport regions in the world in terms of trade, and additionally its airports are strong magnets for personnel, being providers of 80,000 jobs.

ADP has been entrusted with the management and development of this group of airports and aerodromes since 1945, 50 years ago last year. It has an annual turnover of seven billion francs (about US$1.5 billion) and a work force of 7,000 people, which constitutes an extremely valuable human asset in terms of competence and experience in all aspects of airport activity.

ADP not only runs its own airports, but also exports its engineering and architectural know-how around the world by helping in the creation of airports in such places as Abu Dhabi, Jakarta, Kansai, Brunei, Cairo, and Dar es Salaam.

As with any airport authority, ADP has to respond to the needs of the air transport industry as regards the capacity of its installations. It has invested ten billion francs (about US$2 billion) in Orly and Roissy-Charles de Gaulle over the last five years. ADP is also tackling challenges which are arising more than ever before. These include satisfying the clientele, helping the economic development of the Paris region, succeeding in making its airports environmentally compatible, and reinforcing Paris's position as one of the world's largest airport systems.

With all this activity, Aéroports de Paris will be entering the next millennium fully in the tradition of all those who have helped build French aviation into what it is today.

Jean Fleury, President, Aéroports de Paris

Acknowledgements

During the preparation of this book, we have been fortunate to receive help and advice from numerous people associated with the air transport industry in Paris. We thank everyone who so patiently answered our requests for information, and everyone who provided access to the airports and aircraft.

We would particularly like to express our gratitude to the public relations staff and ground crews of Aéroports de Paris, especially Jean Fleury, Paul Andreu, Hector Sberro, Jacques Reder, Yves Le Goff, Catherine Benetreau, Stéphanie Crespin, Solange Dhelens, Annick Girodroux, Isabelle de Langlade, Christine Martin, Bruno Rivière and Gérard Servat.

Cover photos (front): Concorde and (back): Airbus Industrie A340

Copyright © 1996 Pyramid Media Group
First published in the UK in 1996
by Airlife Publishing Ltd.

ISBN 1 85310 776 X

British Library Cataloguing in Publication Data
A catalogue record for this book
is available from the British Library

Text by Aram Gesar
Foreword and history section by Aéroports de Paris
Edited by Robin Bonner and André Bréand
Electronic Production by Craig Williams

Photographs:
© 1977-95 Aram Gesar;
© ADP Aéroports de Paris / Paul Maurer, Bruno Rivière, Jean-Claude Paintendre, Yves Le Goff, Georges Halary, Michel Tiziou, Yannick Ménager, François Jannin, Jean-Claude Flouvat, Gabriel Liesse, Jacques Levavasseur, Philippe Brazil;
© G. Donati.

A book edited and produced for Airlife by
Pyramid Media Group
29 route de Pré-Bois, CP 635
CH-1215 Geneva Airport
Switzerland

Airlife Publishing Ltd
101 Longden Road, Shrewsbury SY3 9EB, England

A Short History of the Airports of Paris

Until 12th November 1906, the elegant public enclosures of the Bagatelle (a racecourse set in a clearing in the Bois de Boulogne, a wood just outside Paris) had only been trodden on by the shoes of the fashionable and the hooves of the trotters. However, on that day, it awoke to the sound of an engine: Alberto Santos-Dumont, Brazilian by birth but Parisian by adoption, was taking off in a fragile biplane he had constructed himself. He managed to cover 220 metres at a height of six metres and in a time of 21.2 seconds. It was the first world record for distance! Right from the first days of heavier-than-air flight, Paris was forging for itself a vocation as a pioneer, a role it still maintains today.

In the months following Santos-Dumont's exploit, the French capital became the site of some of the world's greatest aeronautical achievements. First of all, still in 1906, Louis Blériot flew an ancestor of the seaplane over Lake Enghien. On 13th January 1908, Henry Farman flew the world's first closed-circuit kilometre, above an army exercise lawn in Issy-les-Moulineaux. Further south in Juvisy a few months later, an airfield opened that clearly proclaimed its ambitions: it called itself an Air Port.

On 16th and 17th October 1910, there was another first when Winjmalen of Holland flew with a passenger from Paris to Brussels and back in less than 36 hours. Air transport had been born, albeit modestly.

The Great War put a stop to these early efforts for a while and was to have a lasting effect on the whole future of aviation in the Paris area. At the beginning of hostilities, the French military created an air base in the north-eastern suburb of Le Bourget, the point where German attacks on the capital were considered most likely to occur. And three years later in 1917, the American La Fayette squadron set themselves up in a pasture near the Vieille-Poste Farm at Orly.

With peace restored, Le Bourget was converted into one of the first civil airports in Europe. On 8th February 1919, Lucien Bossoutrot took off for London in a Farman Goliath with twelve passengers on board. Two days later, in a Caudron C23, Georges Boulard headed for Brussels with ten passengers. "Airlines" were multiplying: in 1919, there were as many as 27 serving Paris. The number of air travellers was becoming significant too. In 1920, Le Bourget welcomed 6,280 passengers in the first Parisian "air terminal", a small wooden building. And this despite the fact that at the time, a return ticket to London cost no less than 12,000 francs.

While the pioneers were continuing their brilliant exploits, air travel began to spread more broadly

By the early twenties, Paris was linked by air to most French metropolitan regions and European capitals. In less than five years, air transport had made considerable progress. On 7th June 1922, René Labouchère accomplished the first night flight Paris-London-Paris, in a Goliath with eight passengers aboard, one of whom was the first aviation novelist, Louise Faure-Favier. The new method of transport was starting to spread. The public were getting used to airplanes.

Meanwhile, the pioneers were remaining faithful to their motto: "always further, always higher, always faster". History was being written, sometimes spectacularly. On 24th April 1924, Georges Pelletier Doisy reached Tokyo from Le Bourget in 47 days after 120 flight hours. In 1926, more and more long-distance flights were being undertaken: Paris-Peking (now Beijing) by the same Pelletier Doisy, Paris-Basra by the Arrachart brothers, Paris-Omsk by Girier and Dordilly, and Paris-Tananarive (now Antananarivo) in Madagascar by Jean Dagnaux.

On 21st May 1927 at 10:22 pm, 300,000 Parisians witnessed not a take-off but a landing: that of Charles Lindbergh. He had just crossed the North Atlantic in 33.5 hours in a small single-engine aircraft called the "Spirit of Saint-Louis", in recognition of the financial backing he had received for his exploit from businessmen of that town.

In the early hours of 1st September 1930, thousands of onlookers witnessed the departure for New York of Dieudonné Costes and Maurice Bellonte on board their Breguet "Point d'Interrogation" ("Question Mark", in English). They arrived 37 hours, 18 minutes later.

Other pages of this history, however, were being written in letters of blood. Just a few days before Lindbergh's arrival, Charles Nungesser and François Coli had taken off on their last journey, aboard the "Oiseau Blanc" ("White Bird"), in which they tried unsuccessfully to reach America. And some years later, on 6 December 1936, Jean Mermoz left Le Bourget on board a regular flight to Dakar, where he took command of the mail seaplane "Croix-du-Sud" ("Southern Cross") and headed for Natal in Brazil. He never arrived.

By the end of the 1930s, Paris had one of the most modern airports in the world

In 1930, 55,000 passengers passed through Le Bourget. Air transport was slowly losing its adventurous aspect and was becoming rather routine and even comfortable. The "Golden Ray" service of the Air Union company was offering deluxe catering on its flights, with champagne dinners served by stewards. New airliners were appearing, safer, bigger and faster than their predecessors. The Douglas DC-2, flown by KLM, was the first all-metal plane. This was followed by the Junkers 52 of Lufthansa. Both could carry twenty passengers.

7th October 1933 was a red-letter day for French air transport: it was then that four airlines, Air Orient, CIDNA, Air Union and SGTA — later to be joined by Aéropostale — amalgamated to form Air France. The official ceremony, at which several Farman 303 and Wibault three-engine planes were used as a backdrop, took place at Le Bourget, which then became the operational base of the new company.

One of the first concerns of Air France was to rationalise and modernise its fleet through the acquisition of French aircraft capable of competing with the rival Bloch 220s and Dewoitine 338s. With its cruising speed of 260 km/h, the Dewoitine was nicknamed the "12-passenger racing plane".

The airlines' route-networks began to span the whole world as the numbers of destinations multiplied. From 1935, one could take daily flights from Paris to anywhere in Europe and even North Africa. Airport infrastructures had to adapt to the increasing traffic, and even anticipate it. With the coming of the 1937 Universal Exhibition in Paris, Le Bourget underwent a great transformation. A modern and well-lit terminal, capable of handling 8,000 passengers a day, was built. An extremely well equipped control tower, and concrete runways and taxiways allowed Le Bourget to cope with about 18,000 aircraft movements and 131,000 passengers in the very first year of its operation in its new form.

From 1st May 1939, Le Bourget was operating at night as well as during the day, following the inauguration by Air Bleu, which specialised in carrying mail freight, of night flights to Bordeaux, Lyons and Marseilles.

This night use was made possible by the installation of extremely accurate direction-finding equipment.

By this time, Le Bourget had become one of the world's principal airports, and air transport had become an industry of which Paris was in the forefront. But the War was to change things drastically.

In 1946, Orly was rebuilt with a wooden terminal! In 1960, the airport handled two million passengers

In the summer of 1944, the two Paris airports were in a disastrous state. The splendid terminal at Le Bourget had fallen into ruin. In the ensuing months, it daily received thousands of prisoners of war returning from Germany. Commercial traffic did not resume until 2nd January 1946, when an Air France Douglas DC-4 took off on the airline's first flight to New York.

Meanwhile, the U.S. Army had managed to tidy up the ruins of Orly, and the airport received, beginning in February 1946 even before it had been handed back to the French, the first Lockheed Constellations of TWA. A notable point about the airport at that time was that the passenger terminal was made of wood!

Everything was having to be rebuilt, starting with the business structure of the industry itself. In November

1944, General De Gaulle had received a report, written by a high-ranking and visionary civil servant named Alain Bozel, advising the setting up of an autonomous entity to manage all Paris airports. The idea was acted upon rapidly. On 24th October 1945, "Aéroport de Paris" was created as a public institution charged with the management of all airports or aerodromes within 50 km of the capital.

Before long, Le Bourget had recovered its pre-war aspect. And Orly, which had been a small airport with flying schools and dirigible hangars between the Wars, expanded, acquiring in 1948 a second, more solid terminal called the North Terminal. Five years later, Air France moved to Orly, necessitating the construction in nine months of a new, "temporary" South Terminal. This opened in 1954. In 1960, with 27

French and foreign airlines using Orly, the two terminals handled, with some difficulty, around two million passengers. This was twice as many as Le Bourget, which had been prevented from expanding by the surrounding urbanisation.

The management of Aéroport de Paris had also been preparing for the future. From the mid-50s, Orly became an enormous building site. A 3,300m runway, eventually inaugurated in November 1959, was being constructed. A new, ultra-modern air terminal of a then novel architectural type had been designed: a huge glass and steel building, 400m long. The building would be able to handle six million passengers a year, and its modular construction would allow for future extensions. At the official opening, General de Gaulle paid homage to its creators: "If ever a product could justify the pride of those who made it with their intellect and with their hands, it is this one, which is at the meeting point of heaven and earth."

Progressively, airports became not only interfaces between passengers and planes, but places to stay and centres of economic activity

On 12th September 1958, the first Boeing 707 of Pan Am landed at Le Bourget, and on 24th March 1959, Air France inaugurated its first Caravelle service at Orly. With the coming of jet aircraft, air transport was entering a new era of drastic technological evolution. In just a few years, a complete change of scale was to take place: the jets could offer speeds and capacities twice those of the previous generation of aircraft. The new South Terminal at Orly opened in time to receive

them. And to welcome all the spectators who crowded onto the terraces: although aircraft had become a popular means of transport, they were also still things to dream about. It was the time of "Sundays at Orly", the title of a popular song by Gilbert Bécaud. In 1966, Orly received four million visitors — more than the Palace of Versailles!

But Aéroport de Paris had to confront other needs and challenges as well. With the expansion of air travel created by jet aircraft, air freight was developing too. A freight terminal was constructed at Orly, opening on 19th January 1962, and one was opened at Le Bourget the following summer. The size of the new planes also necessitated new technical installations, such as the giant maintenance hangar, N 3, built for Air France in Orly's north zone. Passengers too made

their desires known. A cinema was installed in Orly South, followed in October 1965 by a Hilton Hotel. Little by little, the airport ceased to be a mere interface between passenger and plane and became a place to stay and a centre of economic activity.

The 1960s witnessed another phenomenon: the explosion of domestic air traffic. Created in 1962, Air Inter experienced a spectacular growth, so much so that very soon the South Terminal proved insufficient to handle the additional activity. In July 1968, the two Paris airports between them had exceeded the symbolic barrier of one million passengers a month. To handle all these extra people, Aéroport de Paris invented a revolutionary concept that would be embodied in a new terminal to be called Orly West. It would involve a new way of parking aircraft for passenger boarding and deplaning, with walking distances reduced to a few dozen metres. This would allow quick transfer to connecting flights, thus providing local passengers with easy access to the whole world. Ten years before the Americans, Aéroport de Paris had invented the famous "hub."

Charles de Gaulle Airport was built in time for the new wide-body planes

Alain Bozel had been truly visionary when, in 1944, he had foreseen the future development of air transport and had suggested transferring all Paris air transport activity to a single huge installation, to be constructed near Saclay. This had not been done at the time, but in 1957, the management of Aéroport de Paris did begin to envisage the creation of a new airport. Le Bourget was unable to expand because of the intense urbanisation around it, and the land

reserves that Orly did have were not significant.

In 1964, Prime Minister Georges Pompidou agreed to the development of the "Paris North" airport on an agricultural site in the Plaine de France, between Le Mesnil-Amelot and Roissy-en-France. The ground-breaking ceremony took place on 1st December 1966. This proved very good timing as only three years later, the first Boeing 747 of Pan Am landed at Orly. The new generation of jetliners, the "Jumbos", were bringing to the air transportation industry the additional problem of size. Many airports around the world would suffer from this situation — but not those of Paris.

While waiting for the opening of the new airport, Orly proved its adaptability. Two satellites with telescopic jetways were added to the South terminal to receive the wide-body planes now using the fourth runway, which had been operational since September 1965.

Paris North had greater ambitions though. The initial plan anticipated a capacity of 50 million passengers a year. Its creators had thought big: 3000 hectares (one third the area of Paris itself!), five runways and five terminals. The first of these terminals, built in September 1968, was unusual in that it was circular, a shape which reduced passenger walking distances and allowed a maximum of planes to be in contact with the terminal.

On 8th March 1974, the new airport at Roissy, by then named "Charles de Gaulle" (or "CDG" in air transport circles) was inaugurated by Prime Minister Pierre Messmer. Two years later, its futuristic shape received the first commercial flight of Concorde.

Aéroport de Paris — which before long was to change its name to "Aéroports de Paris" (ADP) — maintained its effort to keep ahead of the expansion in the traffic. A second terminal, of a different design to the first, was taking shape. It would be modular and more "extrovert". The first two modules were inaugurated in 1981 and 1982 and two more in the following seven years. In 1992, CDG handled 25.2 million passengers — as many as Orly.

A turn-of-the-century airport is served by all forms of transport.

A modern airport gradually becomes like an actual town as it acquires its own roads, shops, services and hotels.

With air transport being centered mainly around business trips, businessmen expect to find all the facilities needed to continue working while waiting for connecting flights. This is a need that is particularly felt at Orly, where frequent use is made of such flights. The first business centre was installed in the South Terminal, with meeting rooms and conference rooms of varying sizes. A similar installation was then opened in Orly West, which includes every type of office equipment, a secretariat, a bar and a meals-on-trays service.

Furthermore, ADP's management wanted to benefit from the large areas of unused land on their airports by setting up industrial, commercial and service activities connected with air transport and themselves capable of increasing the traffic. Thus were born various programs to construct buildings on the airports, either owned by ADP and rented to other entities, or directly owned by separate entities. First there were Entrepots Juliette [entrepots means warehouses] at Orly and Village Fret [freight] at CDG. Also created were facilities for storage, distribution and after-sales service for freight agents and export companies. These were followed by the construction of Orlytech and Roissytech, quality buildings for import-export and office activities. These two buildings cover more than 50,000 square-metres. Additionally, a third such zone is currently being developed at CDG, called Roissypole.

Such an "air city" also has to maintain its other links with the outside world — not just its air links. Staff and passenger movements to and from the airport number tens of thousands a day. To avoid complete congestion of the road traffic networks, ADP had very early on planned for the utilisation of mass transport. As early as 1972, with the help of SNCF [the French national rail organisation], Orly-Rail was created. This was followed in October 1991 by Orlyval, an automated shuttle system linking Orly with an RER line [the RER is the Paris rapid transit system, partly underground and partly above ground]. For CDG, Roissy Rail opened in 1976.

But it was with the opening, in November 1994, of a TGV station [TGV stands for Train à Grande Vitesse, which means high-speed train] under Terminal 2, that CDG became fully integrated with the outside world. By becoming the first major airport in the world to possess a fast rail connection, CDG hopes to attract an extra 500,000 passengers a year.

Air, road, rail and underground: a late 20th-century airport is served by practically all forms of transport.

There is continual open dialogue with the airports' neighbours about pollution and other problems

The area around an airport is continually faced with many problems. First of all, there is the noise, which is an increasing nuisance due to the urbanisation that has been occurring around the airports. In 1895, the village of Orly had 982 inhabitants. Now, just a century later, there are more than 25,000, many of whom settled there long after the opening of the airport. There is a similar situation at CDG, where cereal fields and deserted valleys have rapidly become populated since the mid-70s.

ADP has long been conscious of the problems created by the cohabitation of aircraft and local inhabitants. Over a period of 20 years, more than 450 dwellings situated in the most exposed areas were purchased from their original owners, and some 1400 buildings were given additional soundproofing. Altogether, 500 million francs (about US$106 million) were used for these operations.

Additionally, ADP is constantly upgrading the air traffic system so as to limit the noise problem. The Sonate system ("Suivi opérationnel des nuisances d'avions et de leurs trajectoires pour l'environnement", which means operational monitoring of the harmful effects on the environment of aircraft and their flight paths) monitors flight paths and noise along the axes of the runways. There are four measuring stations at Orly and seven at Roissy. Also, since 1992, the landing fees paid by airlines have been adjusted according to the noise level of their aircraft, and the extra money collected has been used to help the local populace further soundproof their homes. Since 1994, a "Plan de gêne sonore" or PGS [noise disturbance program] has enabled these people to receive an amount of financial assistance calculated according to the relationship of their homes to the sources of the noise.

Air pollution poses less problems. All analyses show that the atmosphere is purer at Orly and CDG than in Paris itself or its suburbs. Even so, ADP has been working to reduce harmful emissions from road vehicles by itself using electric vehicles at both these airports.

The problem of ground-water pollution is also taken very seriously. Before being discharged into the Seine, such water is decontaminated so effectively that it becomes pure enough to drink.

Since 1992, all ecological measures have been combined into ADP's five-year Environmental Plan. This stipulates that ADP will devote 450 million francs (about US$95 million) to the carrying out of several projects to fight pollution and other nuisances. Under this plan, Environmental Offices were created at CDG and Orly. These are places of information and dialogue where ADP can fully present its campaign against pollution, and fully answer people's questions.

Air transport needs impose continuing changes on airports

Among the 142 regular airlines serving Paris and connecting it to a network of 510 cities in 135 countries, many are not doing well financially. This is a consequence of an imbalance between supply and demand which adversely affects revenue. This weakness has a direct influence on the whole of the air transport system, including airports. Like its competitors, ADP is affected by the fluctuations of this strongly cyclical activity, and must therefore continually adjust its actions and investments.

This is not the only challenge. The creation of a united Europe is also bringing its own complications. The liberalisation required by Brussels has created ferocious competition among the airlines of the Old World, which directly influences the activities of airports. The abolition of the earlier constraints against opening new routes or increasing flight frequencies has provoked an explosion in aircraft movements. This new freedom has also applied to the choice of airports served. ADP was obliged to rethink the distribution of traffic between its

two main airports when the European Union required Orly to accept new intra-Community flights. A difficult obligation to satisfy, considering the fact that the French government intends to limit the number of annual movements at Orly to a maximum of 200,000 — a level that has already been reached!

ADP had therefore to completely modify its arrangements with the airlines, including the distribution of these companies between Orly and Roissy. The two Orly terminals will now be utilised in such a way as to make it easier for passengers to catch connecting flights, a facility requested by the airlines. After 35 years of service, Orly South is going to be completely renovated. The West Terminal has already been extended by the addition of Hall 1 in June 1993, and now has the capacity to handle six million passengers a year and the ability to cope with wide-body jets. In all, these changes are costing a total of nearly 600 million francs (about US$130 million).

In the future, Roissy will have to handle most of the increase in Paris's air traffic

Over the last few years, Roissy-CDG airport has been able to handle 320,000 aircraft movements a year, and that with only two runways. An excellent performance, particularly considering that the initial plan envisioned needing no less than five runways to deal with 350,000 movements.

However, in view of the constant increase in Paris's air traffic, and in light of the decision mentioned earlier to limit the number of annual movements at Orly to 200,000, it is CDG alone that will have to cope with the increases.

To prevent the saturation of the current infrastructure at CDG, which would be expected to occur before the end of the century the way things are going at the moment, ADP has planned for the construction of two additional runways, parallel to the existing two. This project, which will have to be agreed to by the relevant political authorities and the elected representatives of the surrounding communities, is currently being studied.

The Ministry of Transport has decided to link the decision process concerning this new runway construction at CDG to a broad study of air traffic in the whole Paris region. A commission has been charged with finding ways to optimize the various modes of transport in the area while at the same time respecting the concerns of local inhabitants, taking into account the respective interests of the Paris "basin" and the nearby French regions, and being in compliance with the requirements of the overall development policy for the area.

It is already time to think ahead to the more distant future when there will be giant aircraft carrying 600, 800 or even 1,000 passengers

ADP's financial situation of can, with justification, seem comfortable, but this is something which is a vital necessity in order to ensure both the growth of the organisation and, above all, its continuing adaptation to the expansion and new demands of air traffic. ADP's last five-year investment program cost over 10 billion francs (more than US$2 billion) but ADP was able to finance virtually all of this from its own resources.

The passenger capacity of an airport and the comfort of its installations are vital aspects of air transport. A new terminal, 2F, is therefore being built at CDG; it will come into service in 1997. It is a geographical continuation of the four existing modules of Terminal 2, and will therefore profit from the experience gained with those to offer, in an architecturally similar structure, a terminal well adapted to end-of-the-century air travel. Its 400-metre length, and its two large "fingers" where the aircraft will park, will allow it to handle ten million passengers a year. And passenger foot circulation will be smooth and fast, with less than 150 metres to cover from the entrance to the boarding gates.

At the beginning of the new century, a second, identical module, CDG 2E, will be built symmetrically with 2F. Together, they will have a capacity of 20 million passengers a year. But it is already necessary to think ahead to the still more distant future, when there will be giant aircraft capable of carrying 600, 800 or even 1,000 passengers. Operations such as booking, boarding and luggage handling will be difficult, while the taxying and take-off of such 600- or 700-ton juggernauts will impose new technical constraints. In compensation, though, the number of aircraft movements at airports should increase at a slower rate.

A modern airport is a major creator of employment and an undisputed factor in economic development

Both as a structural element and an economic driving force, air transport has become in just a few decades an undisputed factor in economic development. And in the future, it will play an even more important role in this domain.

With its 3,000 hectares, Charles de Gaulle airport possesses land reserves undreamed of elsewhere in Europe. These will enable it, in the long term, to have as many as four parallel runways and four terminals to absorb future traffic increases without difficulty. These reserves also allow a great diversification of its air-transport and other activities. Of ADP's total of 6,700 hectares, 600 are reserved for real-estate valorization, i.e., for increasing the value of the land by building factories, business centres, commercial centres, etc., on it.

A modern airport is a major creator of employment. More than 76,000 people work at the two main Paris airports, of which 40,000 are at Roissy. Including indirect employment, there are some 150,000 workers who earn their livelihood from the Paris airports, generating an annual turnover of 130 billion francs (about US$26 billion) per year, or 8% of the Paris region gross domestic product. For every one million increase in the annual number of passengers, more than 1,000 direct jobs need to be created, and as many indirect positions.

But any development must have the problems it causes taken into account. The government has therefore decided to launch an all-embracing study on the future airport needs of the whole Paris region. Should Roissy be allowed to keep growing, or should an upper limit be set? If the latter, and if France does not want to see its position in the world air transport market decline, how should the excess traffic be absorbed? By redistributing it to the big regional airports, or by the construction of a third airport further away from the capital?

Whatever the answers to these questions are, ADP will continue to be faithful to its mission of serving the public, the air transport industry, and the country.

Of revolutionary design when it was built, the huge departure hall on the ground floor of Orly's South Terminal allows easy communication between passengers and airport and airline staff, and facilitates the check-in formalities as passengers head toward the boarding areas.

The network of corridors and glassed-in footbridges
makes it easy for transit passengers, and provides
good access to the boarding areas and terminal exits.

Orly's huge picture windows offer both passengers and visitors interesting views of the tarmac area and of the arriving and departing aircraft.

While awaiting their departure, passengers relax in
the light and spacious boarding areas.

Orly Airport's control tower, a modern-day monolith, pictured in a futuristic against-the-light setting.

From a second tower facing Orly's South Terminal, staff control the aircraft parking areas and inform arriving planes where they should dock.

An Airbus A300 of the French airline Air Inter. The company, which had an average of more than 250 aircraft movements a day in 1995, is the biggest user of Orly, its home airport. An aircraft "movement" is defined as one take-off or one landing. The plane pictured on the facing page is an Airbus A320.

This Fokker 100 of French airline TAT is in the colours of British Airways. BA is now TAT's major shareholder and uses this livery for TAT's international flights. TAT is the second biggest user of Orly and flies French domestic and European routes. In the close-up picture, the right half of the tail airbrake can be seen, in the closed position.

The twin-jet McDonnell Douglas MD-82s of ▶ French airline AOM regularly frequent Orly.

The immense tarmacs and aprons of Orly assist in preparing the aircraft for flight. The Air France plane in the foreground is an Airbus A310. Air France's main home base is Charles de Gaulle Airport, but it is also a big user of Orly. The EAS plane is a Boeing 727 and the other AF plane is a Boeing 747 "Jumbo".

The main French, European and international airlines have made Orly their main point of departure and arrival in France. The plane in the foreground is a McDonnell Douglas MD-87 belonging to Iberia of Spain. The logo on the tail in the middle belongs to Continental Airlines of the United States, next to the right is American Airlines, and to its right is Corsair of France.

The tail logos of commercial planes can add bright splashes of colour to a modern airport. The yellow tail on the right is sporting the more familiar logo of TAT, as opposed to the BA colours shown on page 28 which are now used on TAT's international flights. The logo between the Delta and Air Liberté tails belongs to El Al, the Israeli airline.

Highly qualified ground personnel coordinate the arrival and departure movements of all planes when they are near their parking areas. This plane is a Boeing 737-300 of TAP Air Portugal.

The French regional company Air Littoral flies to
small and medium-sized cities. The plane shown here
is a twin-engine Embraer Brasilia.

The large number of movements of aircraft on the
ground necessitates strict discipline on the part of
drivers of the many road vehicles that are needed on
a modern airport. The plane in the middle is a Boeing
767 of Air Algerie, the Air France plane in the
background is an Airbus A300, and the TAP Air
Portugal and Corsair planes are both Boeing 737s.

Take-off of a Boeing 737 of the national Moroccan airline Royal Air Maroc. In today's environment, the 737 is still known for its reliability, often shuttling passengers on tight commuter schedules and on charter flights. Although a latecomer to the market, orders for this jet have surpassed 3,000, making it the best-selling commercial airliner in the world.

The wide-body Boeing 767s of American Airlines fly between Paris and North America daily. The airline operates a fleet of more than 60 boeing 767 aircraft, a mix of 767-200 and -300, most of them on international routes.

Although it doesn't have a great presence at Orly, the Spanish charter company Viva Air, with its Boeing 737-300s, is very well-known to tourists. In 1984, Boeing introduced the 737-300, first of the advanced technology series. Today, the 737 "family" consists of three sizes of virtually the same airplane, seating from 100 to 170 passengers.

The French charter airline Euralair uses two models of Boeing 737, the -200 as shown here, and the new -500. Boeing also produces two other new-generation 737's, the -300 and the -400. All three incorporate advanced avionics equipment, quieter more efficient engines, and other new technologies. Because they all share the same cockpit layout, any flight crew trained on one model can also fly the other two.

The Russian-made Tupolev Tu-154s of the Rumanian national carrier Tarom used to fly regularly to Orly. The Tu-154 is normally laid out to accommodate 158 to 164 passengers in a single-class layout. It has a range of about 3,000 miles (4,800 km) with a full passenger load. Nowadays they have been replaced by Airbus A310-325s.

An Egyptair Airbus A300 taxying. Egyptair, the flag-carrier of the Arab Republic of Egypt, has chosen the Airbus A340 and the Boeing 777 as part of its commitment to modernize its fleet.

Pakistan International Airlines' fleet includes eight Boeing 747-200s. The different 747 models are easy to identify. The upper deck of the -200 has ten passenger windows each side whereas the -100 has only three each side. Both the -300 and -400 have identical extended upper decks, but the -400 has winglets canted upwards at the ends of the wings, while the -300 does not.

In its Orly workshops, national carrier Air France carries out the maintenance of aircraft of foreign airlines, such as this Tupolev Tu-154 of Armenian Air Lines.

Thanks to the introduction of the Juliette warehouses, thousands of tons of goods pass through the freight terminal every day, coming from or going to every airport in the world. The plane is a Boeing 747-400.

In the freight zone, sophisticated vehicles and pieces of equipment are used to load and unload the planes. Pictured here is a Boeing 747F freighter.

The increasing size and weight of planes has forced manufacturers to equip their aircraft with ever larger and more powerful engines. The most powerful to date is the General Electric GE90 powering the new Boeing 777.

With all its fairings and inspection doors open, an engine is readily accessible to maintenance technicians.

A view of a Boeing 747 that highlights the plane's size. Clearly visible is the exhaust nozzle of the Auxiliary Power Unit (APU), a small jet engine that many modern jet airliners have in order to provide electrical power for the basic functions of the craft when the main engines are not operating.

The unfailing and thorough inspection of the under-carriage and tyres is one of the major tasks of aircrew and runway technicians before each takeoff.

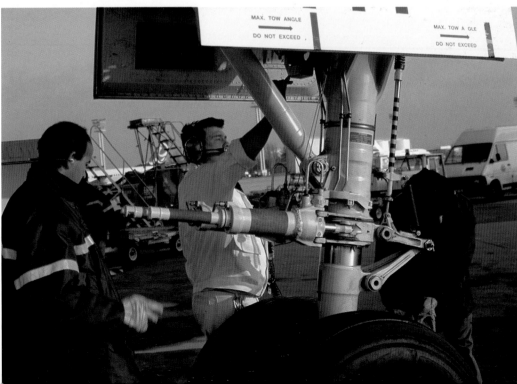

Security and pre-flight inspections are the watchwords of the crew before every flight. The least fault is immediately reported to the technicians who have the power to decide whether or not a plane can take off.

Take-off of one of Delta Airlines' 56 Lockheed TriStars. The airline has a huge fleet of more than 500 aircraft, and flies to Europe, Asia, Canada, and Mexico, as well as domestic routes throughout the United States. Delta also operates Boeing 767-200 and -300 aircraft to Europe.

CHARLES DE GAULLE

An integral part of Roissy-Charles de Gaulle's Terminal 2, the TGV station is an immense cathedral of glass and steel, designed in a deliberately futuristic style. The TGV is the French "Train à Grande Vitesse", which means High-Speed Train.

The bright entrance halls and gate lounges provide a delightful atmosphere for passengers.

Bright, comfortable departure lounges are the
interfaces between the terminals and the departing
planes.

The control tower at Roissy-Charles de Gaulle handles more than 320,000 aircraft movements a year. An aircraft "movement" is defined as one take-off or one landing.

An Airbus A310 of Air France, docked at one of the modules of Roissy-CDG's Terminal 2. Charles de Gaulle is Air France's home base and the airline is the airport's biggest user, with more than 300 aircraft movements a day.

British Airways, the second biggest user of the airport, has a fleet that includes Boeing 767-300ERs like this one. British Airways became a Boeing 777 customer in August 1991, with an order for 15, plus 15 options. Prior to that, BA was one of the group of major airlines that helped Boeing define and develop the 777 configuration.

The French airline Air Inter, as well as being the major user of Orly, also has a considerable presence at CDG. Pictured here is a medium-haul Airbus A320 twinjet. The airline also operates Airbus A321s and A330s from this airport.

A Boeing 737 of German airline Lufthansa, in front of one of Terminal 1's satellites. In 1994, Lufthansa contracted to sell its 32 older model 737-200s to four Indonesian carriers in a $300 million package deal which included a large supply of parts, a flight simulator, and spare Pratt & Whitney JT8D-15 turbofan engines.

Italian airline Alitalia uses McDonnell Douglas DC-9s for its flights between Paris and the main Italian towns and cities. The airline is replacing its DC-9s and MD-80s with Airbus Industrie A320 and A321 aircraft.

The French firm Aéropostale has a fleet of Boeing 727 and 737 aircraft. Its activities include regular airline services, charter flights, and above all the carriage of mail for the French Post Office.

British Midland is one of the many airlines that flies between France and the United Kingdom. This plane is a Fokker 70 twinjet. Pilots refer to the quick-descent approaches of the Fokker 70 and F28 as the "crowbar." This is an exaggerated description of the descent in the "Z" shape of an old-fashioned crowbar.

The main Scandinavian airline, SAS, carries the colours of Norway, Sweden and Denmark far and wide. The aircraft shown are McDonnell Douglas MD-80 series. The airline recently ordered the Boeing 737-600 for its short- to medium-haul flights.

KLM Royal Dutch Airlines, Trans World Airlines
from the United States, Air Gabon and Ireland's Aer
Lingus are a further four of the many international
airlines flying to Roissy-CDG.

A McDonnell Douglas MD-80 of Swissair negotiates
the taxiways of Roissy, between the administrative
buildings and the control tower. Swissair also flies
the Airbus A320 and A321 to Paris.

The all-new Boeing 777 widebody twinjet in the colours of United Airlines, its launch customer. The 360- to 440-seat twin-jet has cost Boeing an estimated $4 billion in development costs. At $120 million each, Boeing will have to sell as many as 300 before breaking even.

The small British regional airline Air UK regularly flies to Roissy-CDG with its twin-turboprop Fokker 50s. This aircraft type holds a 22 percent share of the international market for 40- to 70-seat turboprop aircraft. The company has already secured a total of 200 orders and 22 options for the 50.

As well as international airlines, Roissy-CDG is also served by European regional carriers. This Saab 340 belongs to Swissair's regional subsidiary Crossair, which also flies the Saab 2000 to Paris.

This Fokker 50 is one of the planes that regional carrier Luxair uses to link Luxembourg with European and Mediterranean towns and cities. The airline also flies Boeing 737-400s and -500s.

Air transport has generated a large number of associated activities, as for example the providing of food for the passengers. This is handled by catering companies, of which Servair is one of the principal ones. The plane in the picture is an Airbus A310 of Air Afrique, an airline owned by a large number of African countries and operating out of Abidjan in the Ivory Coast.

Many freight transport companies use Roissy-CDG as their European hub. Such is the case with Federal Express, whose fleet includes more than 150 Boeing 727s like this one. Overall, Fedex has one of the largest fleets of any air carrier in the world, with over 450 aircraft, ranging from single-engine Cessnas up to Boeing 747 freighters.

An Airbus A320 of Air Charter, the charter subsidiary
of national airline Air France. The carrier also
operates Boeing 737-200 and 727-200 Advanced and
Airbus A300 aircraft.

A British Aerospace 146 of Italian airline Meridiana, whose
fleet includes McDonnell Douglas DC-9s and MD-82s.

The Ilyushin Il-86s of Russia's Aeroflot daily ply the Moscow-Paris route. The Il-86 marked a first for a Russian airliner when it was introduced into service in 1982. It was the first Russian-built widebody, with a seating capacity of 350, nine-abreast with two aisles. It was also one of the first Russian-built airliners to have its engines mounted in pods under the wings, most previous planes having had them either mounted at the back of the fuselage or buried in the wing roots.

The Finnish national airline Finnair mainly uses McDonnell Douglas DC-9s and the MD-80 family, but it also has some DC-10s and MD-11s, and two Airbus A300s of the exact same model as the Kuwait Airways plane on the right.

Roissy-Charles de Gaulle is above all an airport for
widebodies. The Boeing 747s of Hong Kong airline
Cathay Pacific land here daily.

A 747 of Air Canada, showing off the company's new colours. The 747 has four main undercarriage legs, each with four wheels.

It is from CDG's Terminal 1 that Northwest Airlines flies out of Paris to the principal American towns and cities. Pictured here is a DC-10. The airline operates DC-10-30 and DC-10-40 aircraft. The Series 40s are long-range versions made for Japan Air Lines and Northwest; they are powered by Pratt & Whitney JT9D engines instead of General Electric CF6-50s.

A DC-10-30 of Brazilian airline Varig. The multicoloured tail logo behind is Philippine Airlines, and the one on the left is Air Afrique. Most DC-10 operators have been purchasing the newer generation MD-11 or Boeing or Airbus long range twins. In December 1995, Philippine Airlines announced a large order of Airbus aircraft, including A330s and A340s.

The tri-jet Lockheed TriStars of the Saudi Arabian airline Saudia are a common sight at CDG. Recently, Saudia decided to buy 29 Boeing 737s, five Boeing 747s and 12 Boeing 777s, as well as 15 MD-11s from McDonnell Douglas – four for cargo and the rest as passenger planes.

One of the five Airbus A340s operated by Air Mauritius. The type is the four-engined (the outer two engines are not visible in the photo) ultra-long-range model of the A330/A340 family, being able to fly 7,560 miles (12,300 km) nonstop. In 1993, a specially equipped A340 flew round the world with only one stop, setting many new records.

Dramatic shot of a Boeing 747, clearly showing the trailing-edge flaps extended for increasing lift and drag during landing. Note the short condensation trails from the outer edges of the outer flaps. Although the 747 is currently the world's largest passenger-aircraft type, it possibly will not be for much longer. Airbus has announced that it is studying the A3XX, capable of carrying 450-800 passengers, and Airbus and Russian aircraft designers have been discussing plans for huge flying wings capable of carrying around 1,000 passengers. It has also been reported that Boeing and McDonnell Douglas have been studying this concept too, the latter in cooperation with the American space agency NASA.

With its impressive cargo hold, the Antonov An-124 Ruslan is the largest production plane in the world. It is a frequent visitor to Roissy-Charles de Gaulle. One example of an even larger version was made in order to carry piggyback the planned Russian space shuttle Buran. That model, the An-225 Mriya (Dream), has a larger wing with three engines each side, an extended fuselage and a modified tail.

An essential player in the life of an airport, the runway vehicle, called a "Flyco" by the initiated, carries out numerous tasks in liaison with the control tower. One particularly important job is to guide taxying aircraft.

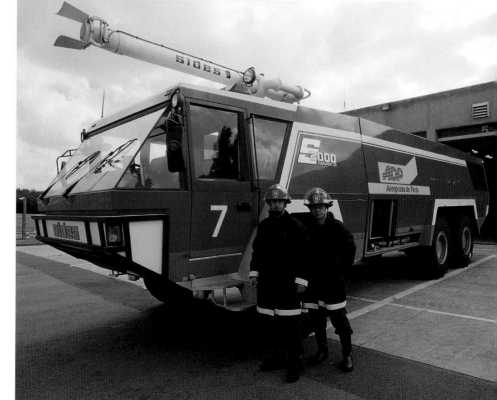

Vital parts of a modern airport, the security services and the fire brigade are prepared for any eventuality. They are equipped with highly sophisticated vehicles and are on alert 24 hours a day.

Maintenance of aircraft and engines is carried out in the technical workshops set up in hangars in the airport's industrial zone, near the terminals. An interesting point in the photo is the unusual type of reverse-thrust mechanism. More commonly, reverse thrust is achieved by deflectors being pivoted into the jet exhaust at the very back of the engine, but the type shown here deflects just the cooler bypass air of a modern jet turbofan.

Aircraft readiness and the regularity of flights are the fruits of many hours of work by the maintenance and ground personnel.

At CDG, planes are fuelled using a fleet of trucks and a complex network of underground pipes and storage reservoirs. The photo is of a Boeing 777, and highlights the very large engine nacelles of this type. This particular aircraft is a United Airlines 777-200, powered by two Pratt & Whitney PW4084 engines. It has a range capability of 4,350 miles (6,960 km).

The undoubted star of Roissy-Charles de Gaulle is ▲ the supersonic Concorde. It flies between Paris and New York every day, to the great satisfaction of business men and women. Concorde cruises at Mach 2, which means twice the speed of sound. Note, in the photo, the condensation in the low pressure area over the wing as the plane lifts off.

CDG's Terminal 2 complex, currently consisting of ▶ Terminals 2A, 2B, 2C and 2D. In the background, work can be seen starting on Terminal 2F, which is due to come into service in 1997, and on its twin, 2E, which will be finished early in the new millennium.

LE BOURGET

Previous Page:
Business aircraft, represented here by these two Gulfstream IV twinjets, nowadays make up the great majority of planes using Le Bourget, which has become the principal airport in Paris for this type of transport.

CHARLES LINDBERGH
APRÈS AVOIR TRAVERSÉ
L'ATLANTIQUE
ATTERRIT ICI LE 21 MAI 1927

LIGUE INTERNATIONALE   DES VIEILLES TIGES
DES AVIATEURS PRÉSIDENT   PRÉSIDENT
CLIFFORD HARMON   LÉON BATHIAT

MISSOURI AIR GUARD

Amongst other things, Le Bourget is famous for its Museum of Air and Space, whose collection of planes, engines and models is one of the most prestigious in the world; and for the fact that every two years, it hosts the International Air and Space Salon. In the early days of aviation, Le Bourget saw many famous and exciting exploits, one example being commemorated by the plaque shown top left. The inscription translates as: "Charles Lindbergh, after crossing the Atlantic, landed here on 21st May 1927." The plane pictured bottom left is a Boeing from the early post-War period. It is a military version of the famous Stratocruiser.

Nowadays, the central building of the old terminal at Le Bourget houses a part of the Museum of Air and Space, as well as service annexes such as the photo library and the documentation service, which is one of the richest in the world.

Some years ago, these famous hangars housed the aircraft maintenance workshops of the French company UTA. Now that UTA is integrated into the Air France group, these workshops are used by independent firms who carry out the maintenance of business aircraft.

Dassault Falcon Service, a subsidiary of Dassault Aviation, rents out a fleet of business aircraft. These planes are often used by insurance companies to fly medical evacuation missions. The plane in the top picture is a twinjet Falcon 2000, and the two craft in the lower photo are trijet Falcon 50s.

An Airbus A300 of national carrier Air France visits Le Bourget to undergo a course of rejuvenation by way of obligatory in-depth maintenance work. Air France carries out such "heavy" servicing at Orly and Le Bourget, as well as at its Toulouse centre, whereas the more frequent "light" maintenance checks are done at Charles de Gaulle.

The BAC One-Eleven twinjet was built as an airliner, but many are now used as business jets. The type first flew in 1963 and a total of 230 were built in the UK, with a few more being assembled in Romania from UK-supplied kits. The aircraft is powered by Rolls-Royce Spey turbojets and the largest model has a maximum passenger capacity of 119. Some One-Elevens have been equipped with water injection for increased power on take-off, a technique that is also used on some Boeing 707s and 747s.

From business jets to charter activities, Euralair has built a solid reputation in the area of transport on demand. Its aircraft range from a four-seat Beechcraft Baron 96, through twinjet business craft such as this Cessna Citation V, to the Boeing 737s as pictured earlier in this book and to Airbus A330 widebody jets. Euralair also has two Boeing 777s on order.

As the home of business aviation in Paris, Le Bourget has shaped its destiny efficiently. The airport has created many jobs connected with this very specialized activity.

Well established at Le Bourget, business-aircraft company Air Entreprise has a modern fleet and is able to respond rapidly to firms needing transport for their executives and directors.

A Boeing 707 modified for private use. The 707 was first flown in 1957 and a total of 1,012 were produced. The last civil version was built in 1979, but military variants were made until 1992. These included many E-3 Sentry AWACS (airborne warning and control system) craft. Currently, E-8 J-STARS (joint surveillance target attack radar system) planes are being created, but these are conversions of existing civilian 707 airframes.

Of similar configuration to the Boeing 707, the Douglas DC-8 first flew in 1958. In 1966, Douglas stretched the fuselage by nearly 37 ft (about 11 m) to produce the DC-8-60, which had a maximum passenger capacity of 269. Later, 110 of these were converted to DC-8-70s by re-engining them with CFM56 turbofans, and the aircraft in the photo is one of these.

Inside huge hangars, teams of technicians renovate and recondition aircraft coming under new ownership.

This Boeing 747, now retired due to high flight time, is being used for spare parts. It has been painted with an anti-corrosion coating to protect it from the elements.

A Lockheed C-130 Hercules, the West's most widely used military transport. More than 2,000 have been produced, and they are in service in over 60 countries. The type, which is powered by four Allison turboprops, first flew in 1954 and new versions are still being manufactured and developed. These include the C-130J, which is being made at Lockheed Martin's Marietta works.

Up, up and away in a Canadair Challenger 601. The pre-production model of this aircraft first flew on 8th November 1978, but new versions are still being developed. One of these is the Global Express, which is due to make its first flight in September 1996. It will have an ultra-long range, and be capable of carrying up to 30 passengers.

AERODROMES OF PARIS

As well as running the three main Paris airports, ADP (Aéroports de Paris) also manages several aerodromes in and around the capital.

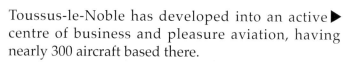

Saint Cyr, above and inset, is, like the other Paris ▲ aerodromes, home to aero clubs and flying schools.

Toussus-le-Noble has developed into an active ▶ centre of business and pleasure aviation, having nearly 300 aircraft based there.

The 116-acre aerodrome of Chavenay, in ▲ west Paris, handles more than 100,000 aircraft movements a year.

With 156,000 aircraft movements a year, Lognes is the most ▲ active of the Parisian aerodromes.

Created in 1905, Issy-les-Moulineaux ▲ ▶ was the first ever Paris airfield. Close to the centre of the capital, it is nowadays used exclusively as a heliport. The businesses operating here are public service and commercial transport companies, who use an impressive fleet of machines.

FOREIGN AIRPORTS

ADP, the Aéroports de Paris organisation, has also been extremely successful in exporting its abundant know-how about airports to countries around the world.

In 1985, the new international ▶ airport of Jakarta-Soekarno-Hatta in Indonesia opened to traffic. ADP had drawn up the overall plan, directed the studies and overseen the work. The airport has two terminals, each of which has seven satellites.

◀ ADP planned the terminal extension at Bandar Seri Begawan Airport in the Sultanate of Brunei, and managed its construction. The extension, which was inaugurated in 1987, is surmounted by the control tower and has a capacity of 1.5 million passengers a year.

Model of terminal proposed by ADP for the airport of Bangkok in Thailand.

◀ Model of the terminal that ADP has proposed for Manilla airport in the Philippines.

Model of ADP's proposal for the future airport of Spata, near Athens, Greece.

ADP conceived and created Abu Dhabi International Airport in the United Arab Emirates. The architecture of the airport, which opened in 1982, fulfils the wish for it to blend well with its surroundings, and for it to be suited to both the climate and the local culture.

القادمون

Arrivals

Conceived by ADP, the terminal of the international airport of Casablanca-Mohammed V in Morocco entered service in 1980. Built in the form of a curve, the terminal has a capacity of three million passengers a year and has docking positions for nine aircraft.

Map of Paris Region Showing All ADP Airports and Aerodromes

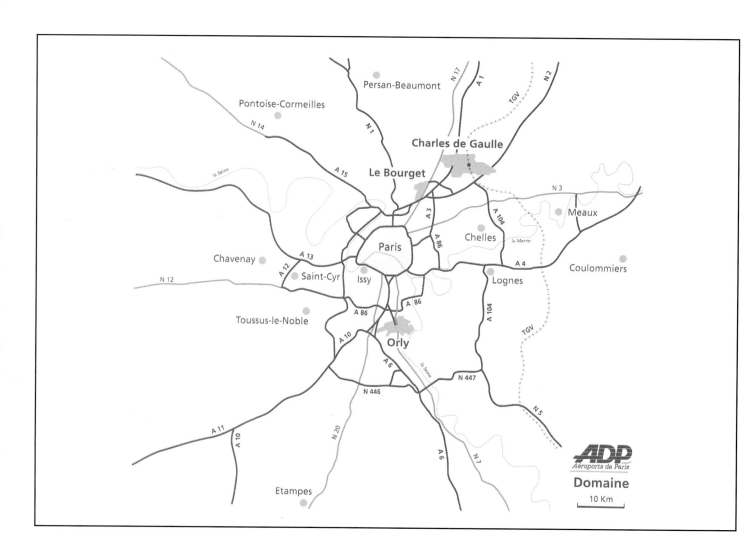

Map of ORLY

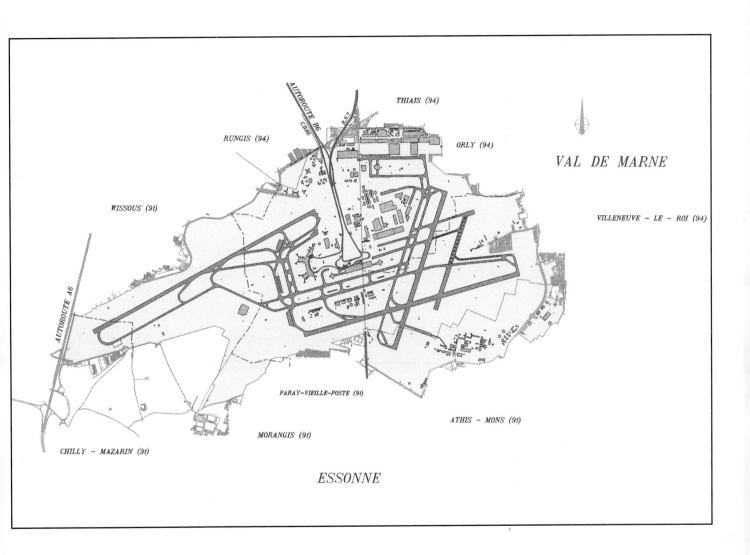

Map of ROISSY-CHARLES DE GAULLE

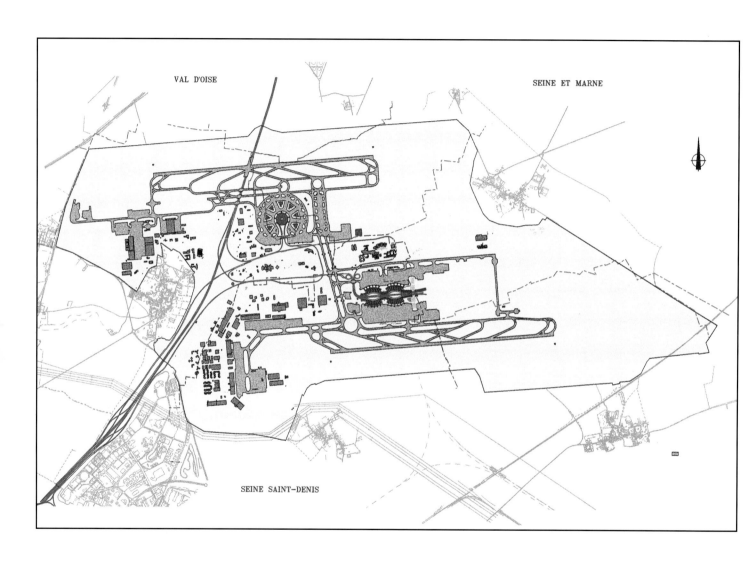

Map of LE BOURGET

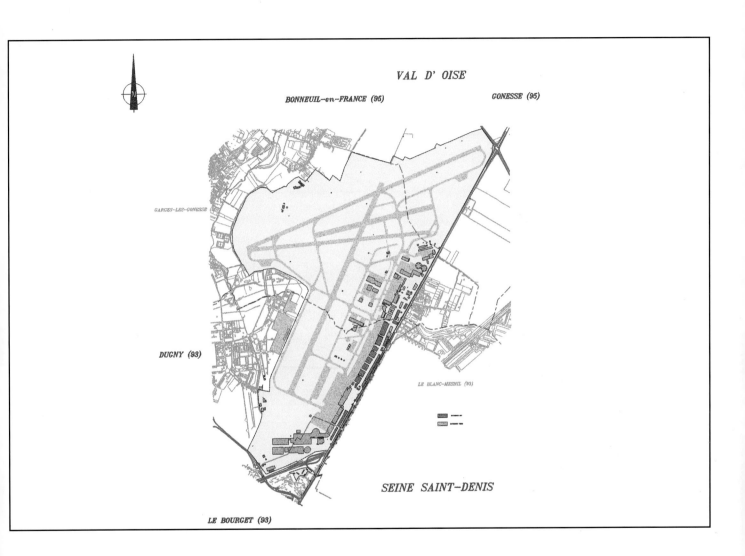

VAL D' OISE

BONNEUIL–en–FRANCE (95)

GONESSE (95)

GARGES–LES–GONESSE

DUGNY (93)

LE BLANC–MESNIL (93)

SEINE SAINT–DENIS

LE BOURGET (93)

Traffic Figures for Orly and CDG Combined

PRINCIPAL RESULTS FOR 1995

Commercial Traffic	1995	95 / 94
Aircraft Movements		
France	180,842	+13.67%
European Union	238,809	+4.00%
Other countries	138,407	-0.45%
Total international	377,216	+2.32%
Total commercial traffic	558,058	+5.74%
Passengers		
France	17,995,214	-0.16%
European Union	17,199,219	-2.70%
Other countries	19,378,195	+1.14%
Total international	36,577,414	-0.70%
Transit	436,554	-0.44%
Total commercial traffic	55,009,348	-0.52%
Freight in Tons		
France	80,099	-12.78%
European Union	123,729	-8.73%
Other countries	896,601	+5.05%
Total international	1,020,330	+3.16%
Total commercial traffic	1,100,429	+1.81%

Market Shares of Top Ten Airlines

	Aircraft Movements		Passengers (excl. transit)		Freight	
1	Air France	23.7%	Air Inter	27.0%	Air France	53.8%
2	Air Inter	20.3%	Air France	24.7%	FedEx	5.8%
3	British Airways	5.4%	AOM	4.3%	Air Inter	4.4%
4	Lufthansa	3.6%	British Airways	4.2%	Air Canada	1.9%
5	TAT	3.4%	Air Liberté	3.4%	American	1.9%
6	AOM	3.2%	Corsair	2.3%	Aéropostale	1.8%
7	Alitalia	2.4%	Lufthansa	2.1%	Cathay Pacific	1.8%
8	Air Liberté	2.4%	Alitalia	2.1%	Japan Airlines	1.6%
9	British Midland	1.9%	British Midland	1.3%	United	1.4%
10	Aéropostale	1.7%	Air Charter	1.2%	AOM	1.4%

Simply *Jersey*

This book is a collection of photography from around our small, but perfectly formed, Island. - a beauty that is *Simply Jersey*.

© Channel Island Publishing

ISBN   978-1-905095-21-X

An artist paints the scene at Mont Orgueil Castle

A Condor Ferries catamaran passes Corbière Lighthouse

The colourful gardens at St Brelade's Bay

Calm waters in St Aubin's Harbour

The world famous Jersey Cow

Clouds gather to replace the sunshine at St John

Elizabeth Castle from the air

An idyllic setting through the trees at Portelet Bay

A beautiful morning at Anne Port

Pink flowers cover the ground at Corbière Lighthouse

Reflections in the sea at St Aubin's Harbour

In the shade at St Peter's Valley

High tide at Ouaisné

La Caumine à Marie Best, St Ouen (Also known as St Peter's Guard House and The White Hut)

A sunny but windy day at St Ouen's Bay

Wild flowers cover the common above Ouaisné

High tide at St Brelade's Bay

Early evening colours at Portelet

As cute as ever - a Jersey calf

A packed beach at Grève de Lecq

St Catherine's Breakwater stretches out towards France

A couple take a stroll near West Park, St Aubin's Bay

Good sailing weather off Corbière Lighthouse

Bonne Nuit Harbour is popular with locals and visitors

Ramblers on a cliff-path above Bouley Bay

Jersey calves explore their new field

The sun goes down on Elizabeth Castle

La Rocque sunset. Note the aircraft vapour trails lit up in the sky

Archirondel with St Catherine's in the background

Portelet Bay provides a peaceful haven for many boats

Beach volleyball at the Gunsite Slip

A busy weekend at St Brelades Bay

Looking down the hill to Mont Orgueil Castle

A ferry passes Elizabeth Castle just after sunset

Bouley Bay from the air

The little harbour at Bouley Bay

Peeping through the trees at Rozel Harbour

Jersey calves standing in the sunshine

The statue of King George V in Howard Davis Park

A lazy Summer's day in Howard Davis Park

Gorilla at Durrell Wildlife

Andean Bear at Durrell Wildlife

Looking down from the hill at the little harbour in Rozel

Inquisitive Jersey cows

Pleasure craft in front of The Boat House, St Aubin

A colourful scene at St Aubin's Harbour

St Brelade's Parish Hall at St Aubin

The Windmill at St Peter

Corbière Lighthouse with a choppy sea

Looking down on Bonne Nuit Harbour

The Elms (National Trust for Jersey)

Jersey calves jostle for attention

A fine, sunny day at St Ouen's Bay

Howard Davis Park with St Luke's Church in the background

Gorey Harbour on a sunny afternoon

St Aubin's Harbour with St Aubin's Fort and St Helier in the background

A boat makes its way out of the Old Harbour, St Helier

A lazy Summer's day on the beach at St Brelade

Palm trees and sunbathers at Havre des Pas

Late Summer in a field at St Ouen

Mother and baby are doing well

Archirondel and St Catherine's Breakwater with the French coast clearly visible in the background

Boats covered for Winter in Gorey Harbour

La Rocco Tower in St Ouen's Bay

A splash of colour at Havre des Pas

La Rocco Tower at St Ouen's Bay

Mont Orgueil Castle (Mount Pride)

It's all action at Gorey Harbour

Surfing at sunset. St Ouen's Bay

Ice plants in front of Corbière Lighthouse

Red Hot Pokers across the bay from Bonne Nuit Harbour

There are many ways to enjoy the footpath leading from Mont Orgueil Castle

Translucent water at Portelet Bay

Youngsters and tourists enjoy the pier at St Brelade's Bay

Lots of colourful umbrellas at St Brelade's Bay

Hobie Cats in St Aubin's Bay

Grève de Lecq from the air

Jersey cows in a typical country setting

Mont Orgueil - a stunning example of a medieval castle

Corbière Lighthouse on a shimmering sea

Visitors relax in the gardens overlooking St Brelade's Bay

A Condor Ferries catamaran passes L'Île au Guerdain

Everyone's enjoying themselves at the Battle of Flowers

Santa must feel hot on this splendid August day

A busy afternoon at St Helier Harbour

Hobie Cats at the Gunsite Slip

Petit Portelet from Mont Orgueil Castle

Gorey Harbour from below the Castle

Late afternoon at Le Hocq

Sunset at Grosnez Castle

The gorse is in flower above St Ouen's Bay

Rozel Harbour on a sleepy Summer morning

Crashing waves at Havre des Pas

A boat crosses the mirrored water in St Aubin's Harbour

Spring flowers in front of Mont Orgueil Castle

Chill out time at La Caumine à Marie Best

Boats tied up at the west end of St Brelade's Bay

A carpet of flowers at Grosnez Castle

The sandy vista of St Brelade's Bay

Another Summer's evening at La Haule Slip

High and dry on the Royal Bay of Grouville

St Ouens Bay from the hill at L'Etacq

The end of the day at La Caumine à Marie Best, St Ouen

Sunset at Corbière Lighthouse

A lone surfer leaves the water as the sun goes down over St Ouen's Bay

The Royal Square at Christmas